THE POWER OF RECOGNITION

PROPHET D. K. AKINBOYE

THE POWER OF REGNITION

ISBN: 9798848194616

Tel: +2348036526319

TABLE OF CONTENT

DEDICATION

To the Holy Spirit my senior partner in the Ministry. By whose grace we have obtained mercy and gained entrance into the power of recognition.

ACKNOWLEDGEMENT

I am very grateful to God who has spared my life and saved my soul to be useful to the kingdom of God in preaching His

Gospel with signs and wonders and inspiring me to write this book.

I cannot but appreciate the effort of all my co-workers in the Ministry, all my Pastors together with all the assistances Pastors.

Moreover, I'm deeply indebted to Pastor Sunday Vincent Akeredolu who assisted me in typesetting the manuscript before the publication.

I also acknowledge the effort of the following people for their support, Dr. (Mrs) O. Obateru, Mr and Mrs Kolawole Peter, Mrs Ilori Morenike and Mr and Mrs Oyeniyi.

Behind a successful man, there is a woman. I really appreciate the presence of my beloved wife, Mrs. Blessing Akinboye and my Children; Samuel and Joy for their support and even allowing me to carry out this project.

INTRODUCTION

It is real that the spiritual controls the physical, likewise our physical manifestation is been controlled by supernatural power.

The Bible says "For though we walk in the flesh, we do not war after the flesh: (For the weapons of our warfare are not carnal, but mighty through God to the pulling down of strong holds)" 2 Corin. 10:3-4.

This signifying that our physical life is taking its source from the spiritual realm.

This book has unveiled the power behind recognition, that it is not just natural people that are valued and highly placed in the society. They are also people that has taken their time to study the scope of life and that are ready to pay the price.

This book comprises a lot of research and spiritual insight on how someone can be recognized both in the kingdom of God and in the society as a whole. Also, this book is not only meant for Church use but also for secular use.

The mystery behind recognition were well exposed in this book. To be recognized in the society is to be reckon with and be a reference point.

CHAPTER 1
WHO AM I?

This is a question that every individual person on earth should ask him/herself. Jesus Christ our Lord asked His disciples this question in Matt. 16:15. Why is He asking such question? Is it because He doesn't know himself personally? No! It is not, but he wants to show to them how important it is to know oneself as that always determine the ability to be known. God was able to be the Ruler of the whole universe because He knows Himself to be God, that always brings about His sovereignty, power, authoritative decision and His manifestation over all creature (Isa. 40:18, 25; 45:5; 42:8). Your potential can only come out when you recognize who you are in God. You can likewise know yourself today if you are ready to recognize God. Your best can only come out when you recognize yourself.

Who am I? Is a personal question that nobody on earth can just answer without the knowledge of Almighty God that created you (Jer.1:4). He knows you before you were born; therefore, nothing is hidden from Him. It is a must that whoever that wants to know him/herself must first know God the Creator of mankind and destiny. It is only God that can disclose your ability unto you, whether you can do it or not (Judges 6:14). When Gideon felt dejected and inferior, it was God whom he knows that told him who he is. You cannot know your ability when you don't know God. Ability to know one remains in God's ability. Joseph knew himself when he gave his life to God and denounced sin which was so easy to stick to Him and was known throughout his generation (Gen. 39:9-11). Cain, Reuben, Esau in Gen. 4:7-8; 49:3-4; 27:40 were unable to reject, neglect sin, deviate from sin, and flee from fornication, youthful lust, and immorality. Hence, failure to listen to God's instruction always brings them lower on the face of the earth and some carry curses that humiliate their glory despite the fact that they were born as a leader and to be known. The greatest problems in life when you don't know yourself it always result to misbehavior, irrational conduct and uncontrollable action/ speech.

CHAPTER 2
THE SECRET BEHIND JOSEPH CLOTH IS WHO I AM

One of the greatest enemies that will not allow you to succeed in life- is inability to identify oneself before you talk of devil. Devil cannot get over you once you know yourself but he can only try you that's for sure. Try to know yourself because the realization about yourself will bring your actualization. People can only demand for you when you actualize your potential. People don't demand for fools that know little about their life.

Joseph was able to become the prime-minister in Egypt because he knew who he was. The intention of Jacob was not ordinary when he made a tunic of many colours for Joseph (Gen 37:3). Please, know fully that it is not the dreams that cause hatred for him but the secret behind his colour. Many may hate you and disregard you when you identify yourself out of many people by knowing who you are and run away from sin.

Benefits of Knowing Who You Are

i. It will assist you and guide you to protect your future from sins that can bury your glory. (Job.31:1).

ii. It will also save your life from going astray from the plan of God and it doesn't matter how long you have gone astray but when you know it try to go back to the right track, you will be relevant.

iii. You can only give the best when you know that what you are doing is what you are expected to do or sent to do. (John 2:1-10).

iv. Knowing yourself will assist you to know your worth and preserve yourself and not to misuse yourself wherever you find yourself.

v. It has been known through all ages that knowing oneself will always command respect to you after actualization but it normally affects the way of thinking about life, the way we dress at times, the way we relate with people and the way we talk and composure.

Your best cannot come out without self-actualization, Joseph regards the honour his father gave to him through his special cloth and behaves distinctly amongst his people truthfully. Joseph operated as a priest by reporting the bad deeds of his brothers without being made a priest because he knows himself. You can only have focus in life when you identify yourself.

Please, knowing fully that a dream or vision that is yet to come to pass is yet to become a mission and a mission that is yet to be fulfilled can never be appreciated or known. Try to work out your dreams in fear of God. Interestingly, it is not the partnership embracement of prodigal son with pigs that called for his repentance but his ability to discover his personality (Lk. 15:1721).

Oh yea sinner! Do you really know that you are losing a lot of divine opportunities, security and benefits you are paying for everyday and a lots of people are begging for promotion with their back on bed of fornicators before they get their assistance (Eph 2:12). It is high time you realize yourself in order to recover all.

If you can give your life to Jesus Christ and everything you are seeking for when you refuse to seek God first belongs to your maker (1 Chron 29:11; Ps. 24:1; 1156). Reasoning of who you are will create a sense of responsibility in you and also assists you in handling life well.

You can only know the importance of existence when your guided dreams is coming to pass as a believer. Oh yea believers resist temptation! It is not for you to just believe in God alone but for your dreams to come true, you need to discipline yourself and knowing that agents of darkness around you will tempt you and bring you down if care is not taken (Pr. 1:10).

Don't allow devil to make prey of you because you are more than what people think you are. It is not an error, they don't know what you know, they don't hear what you heard and they don't see what you have seen, therefore they may not know you, but what you know about yourself will determine how important your life will be to you

CHAPTER 3
WHAT AM I CREATED FOR?

This is all about our assignment in the world. It is not only what you are that will amount to your destiny but also what you are sent to do in the world. You must identify the purpose of your coming and living in the world.

It is what you are known for doing they will call you to do. It is your profession that will call people to respect you, recognize you and even call for your attention.

Identification of your career or job will guide your focus in life. And you can only succeed on what you are divinely assigned to do in life when you know it in time.

Samson's profession was inquired from the angel of the living God (Judges 13:12). John the Baptist assignment was foretold also before his birth that necessitated his living in the wilderness before he started his full ministry (Luke 1:13-17). Mere knowing your assignment beforehand will assist you to keep your vision alive.

Methuselah lived 696 years on earth without the record of achievement in life mainly because he didn't know his purpose in life.

Josiah assignment in the world was prophesied through the young prophet in Bethel in Kings 22:1; 23:16-18. You must know surely that what God planned for you from the onset of the world can only be fulfilled when you are currently in the programme of God not as an unbeliever or a backslider.

We should all know that the programme of God for man's life is not automatic but conditional as you obey Him (Jer 18:7-10; Jonah 3:9; Jer 42:10; Heb. 10:38; Ezek 18:24).

Mary was very sure that Jesus Christ could perform wonder in the marriage of Cana of Galilee even though she has never seen Jesus Christ doing that before but she said to the disciples that whatever He says to you do (John 2:1-10). You can only produce your best in what you are assigned to do on earth more than anybody else that doesn't have a divine backing as regard what they are doing in life.

CHAPTER 4
YOUR GEOGRAPHICAL LOCATION

It is not only what you are and your assignment in the world that will amount to your destiny but also your geographical location. You can only be known, secure, proposer, succeed and victorious in where God wants you to be.

It is very necessary for us to know exact location for our destiny and stop beating about the bush. Don't be ignorant of this view in the Bible that wherever your feet step into 'I will take it for you'. It is only the place He has for you that He will take for you (Jos 1:3; Act 1:8).

Some people in the Bible were known with a particular place, not that they were not going elsewhere for ministration or works. Jesus Christ –Mount Olive (Matt. 26:30), Elijah-Mount Carmel, Noah-Mount Ararat, Abraham-Mount Moriah, and Moses-Mount Horeb/Sinai (Exo 3:1).

You must identify the place of your settlement. God is at every place but He has a settled domain for Himself (Ps 48:1-2; 132:1314; 134:2-3; 123:1; 115:16).

Let us reason on how to live our life. Many people today have achieved a lot before in their endeavour and later become nothing and end up having nothing, like "Lot" through incident, war, crisis, and persecution. Lot chooses for himself a land that God will still destroy in future time though he has prospered earlier in life. The place he choose for himself was not a place that God has for his destiny to be fully fulfilled peradventure he asked from God (Gen. 13:17-18). Don't ever choose a place for yourself because of the physical things you see around.

What you see as good thing today may not be good at the end, what you see as joy today may bring sadness tomorrow. But let God order your steps as He ordered the steps of Paul and Silas (Acts 16:6-10). Your assignment is geographical in regard to time factor, ability, your knowledge, your maturity and your mandate to particular set of people (Matt. 10:5).

Jesus Christ was identified with Nazareth because he was taking to the place and this titled His name.

Some people today are not moving forward in where they were living because God doesn't want the place for them and some refuse what God wants for them because of what they were hearing about the place (Isa. 1:19). God talked about willingness and obedient, it is not only for you to obey God's Word and stay in the place but you must desire, love and create an interest in where-ever

He dictates for you and that is the only secret behind a good successful endeavour and it will make you to eat good of the land.

CHAPTER 5
YOUR COMPANION

Your companion can be your relative, spouse, friends, neigbour, mate, apprentice house-helper, and those you move with or doing things with. Your companion can either make or mar your life. Your companion can either build or scatter your life. Your companion can either promote or demote your life, your companion can either elevate or depress your life ***"He that walketh with wise men shall be wise but a***

Companion of fools shall be destroyed" (Prov 13:20)

It is very important that we must know the type of people we are moving with. People can easily say something about you if they see the type of people you are moving with. Every human being born into this world carries their own peculiar covenant that will affect their generation as regards the purpose of God over their life. Don't be a novice, some people also have mingled with devilish covenant and that can also affect their generation negatively. It will be so disastrous or detrimental to your destiny if you are moving with somebody that carries God's curse or punishment.

Many wouldn't have made it or be blessed if not because of their companion. Joseph was born, blessed by God and favoured, and because of God's favour with him, Potiphar was able to receive God's benefit and enjoyment for the sake of Joseph. I am believing we have a lot of children like that in many families of the unbeliever and they may not be able to explain how their blessings comes, not knowing that it is because of the covenanted child of God (Gen. 39:1-5).

Also Laban discovered through his experience that he was blessed for the sake of Jacob (Gen. 30:27). You must take time to study your life and the other people living around you. Jesus Christ influenced the life of the apostles positively through His own covenant. Both Peter and John were highly favoured and impacted through Jesus Christ. People could see the reflection of Jesus Christ in their lives (Acts 4:13), which is a direct covenant of Jesus Christ (Jn. 7:15).

Lot received blessing through the covenant of blessing that God made with Abraham. And he was able to prosper like Abraham even though he wasn't the original man that received the blessing (Gen. 13:5-8).

It is better for you to know those people that their life will support or assist your life. May lives were saved for the sake of Paul (Acts 27:20-25). Relationship is not just free but it has a purpose. It is either positive or negative. Many lives have been jeopardized because of their companion, may be through their evil covenant, instruction, counsel, relationship and action.

Whoever you come across, make sure you make an impact in their life. Those that made a journey with Jonah highly regretted because he was the source of their stormy sea (Jonah 1:1-17). Listen, don't stay where you cannot be celebrated and appreciated. Rejection and hatred is a powerful arrow that can cut off human's life prematurely. Don't make a pit for your enemy for you don't know who will fall into it.

CHAPTER 6
WHO DOES HE CREATED FOR YOU?

This is the grace of God to an individual Christian on earth to recognize his/her spouse or God's given husband and wife.
You cannot just marry anybody you see or any Christian you know. ***"Jesus saith unto her, Go, call thy husband, and come hither. The woman answered and said, I have no husband. Jesus said unto her, Thou hast well said, I have no husband: For thou hast had five husbands; and he whom thou now hast is not thy husband: in that saidst thou truly"*** (Jn. 4:1618). To everybody, it has been known as a will of God. You can only be accounted as a real son of God when you are ready to obey and submit to His will. Many are ready to serve God but don't want to obey when it comes to the place of marital aspect because of their carnality.

Let us take patient to know the mind of God on whom He has selected or chosen for us in life. It is a bad confession and sign whenever you say, you cannot receive or you are not receiving anything from God. As a real genuine child of God, you must know how God is relating with you (Jn. 10:14-16).

You may be a graduate and God may decide to give you an uneducated person and that is the best to Him. Try to know that God doesn't look at physical appearance (1 Sam 16:7). Your best may be the worst in His sight and His best may seems worst to you. God is so different in everything to us (Isaiah 55:8-9). God knows the best for you and He knows everything and that brother you see or the sister you see has been equipped by God Almighty to meet up with all challenges that will rise up in the future time.

The mystery behind the sleeping of Adam when God was creating Eve was the mystery behind the law of agreement, cooperation, understanding (1 Peter 3:7), supportive (Prov. 31:1029), tolerance, compatibility (Amos 3:3), and expectance. It is a must that when God dictates somebody to you, the love must germinate instantly if the love is not there before (Rom. 5:5). God can never give you somebody that will not be compatible with you. We must try to know that out of the 3 types of loves we have in life, **Eros** (relationship love), **erotic** love, (sexual love), and **agape** love (God's love), it is only the agape love that is the true love which is biblical and considered as the best.

This compatibility arrangement by God is what we called ***"the will of God"*** while the human's arrangement is called ***"match making"***. You are not fulfilled until when you are in the programme of God. It is only programme by God from ages till now that you are only attached to a single man and woman though there are lots of mistakes committed by our fore-fathers that was mentioned by Jesus Christ in Matthew 19:5-12.

Whoever He made for you dictates a lot on your glory accomplishment in life. Try to wait on God to know whom He created for you. Don't ever make your own choice. It is a sin for you to reject anybody on the platform of disability (Isa 46:10). God knows everybody and even what we can do in the future. He is our manufacturer and if we want to function well in life, we must try to submit to the authority of Creator through His guided instruction (manual) that we know as logos and rhema. The selection of God is really base on our different or individual temperament. You can never condole or tolerate a temperament that is not arranged for you. If you want to do this through your head-knowledge you will later end up missing your target and goal and eventually miss heaven.

CHAPTER 7
WHO AM I CREATED FOR?

This is all about our marital life. It is a great offer to see you being responsible in life for both the family and to the other people in society. One of those things that bring revolution into his world is studies. Therefore, it is highly important that we must study our spouse in everything to know his/her weakness (not of sin). The journey of being together (couple) is more than to bear fruit alone (children) but great of all is to have a fulfilled destiny and make heaven at last. Many wouldn't have been a prey today but they reject the divine message of God than to pray for divine will of God on the mind of "I want to marry a millionaire or somebody who is so noble in society". Don't be carnal, for to be carnally minded is a sin (Rom 8:16). The secret behind polygamous act in many homes and prostitution is the inability to wait on God for His will. Let it be known to everybody that to marry the will of God doesn't isolate you from the challenges of life. In Mathew 7:24-29, it is both houses that must face the stormy challenges. Many facts are in the Bible that people are not putting into consideration as regards life continuity. You must know that coming together is to necessitate procreation, profitability, friendship, avoidance of loneliness, for fellowship and sexual enjoyment. Staying off from your partner, in the name of travelling oversea, long vacation with parents after being married, is dangerous.

You men, don't try to misuse your headship authority (Eph 5:21-24) by turning your wives to slaves, please see her as your own blood relation (Eph 5:33), even as yourself. Try to encourage them on whatever good they are doing at home and only correct them with love on whatever wrongs you see them doing. All these will promote love and unity in the home (Ps. 133:1-3). Anything you see the woman doing that is okay should be spoken out to allow flexibility and free conscience. Don't try to repay evil for evil on any offence.

Knowing your husband or wife may seem simple to you but your degree of compatibility will dictate much on your life and even in your generation. Please don't rush into marriage because you have heard from God. We still have a lot of things that are there like income of the men and the women that will speak about their physical well-being, don't try to spiritualize this, it is a must. Anybody that will build up a house must first plan for the materials needed before building it up at all (Heb. 3:4). All their orientation should be changed through an experience of a godly counselor. Turning them from boy to man and girl to woman before embarking on marriage, because marriage is for man and woman not boys and girls (Gen 2:24), yet we still have baby husband and wife misbehaving in the home as a result of their unrefined behaviours or background. You cannot force anybody to behave like you but you can pray to change anybody to your own desirable will and by expressing love to your opponent, bearing their weakness, telling him/her your mind. It is true that human's needs are insatiable but the grace of God can be release for his sufficiency in your family. It is also real and factual that whom you are will dictate whom God will give to you (Prov 18:22; 19:14; Ps 18:25-26). Make sure you prepare for your marriage before getting married because your preparation will determine your experience in marriage and don't prepare when you are into it.

CHAPTER 8
HEARING FROM GOD

It is a divine grace for an individual Christian to hear from God. It is an ability released by God for us Christians to recognize the way God is communicating with us. It is very compulsory that you must be hearing from God to show that you belong to Him (Jn 10:15-17). One of the major problems facing some Christians today is inability to discern the way God is relating with them (Job 33:14). It is God's desire that we must be hearing from Him every day to prefect our lives. The will of God for man is to put him through and guide him on every instruction needed to live a fulfilling life.

Adam and Eve were so familiar with the presence and the voice of God (Gen 3:8) but not that they were seeing God physically as some people think. But they were cut off from the grace when they failed to obey the instruction relayed by God's voice.

Hearing from God is termed to be lead of the Spirit. Hearing from God should be a practical living experience that every Christians should have. God can choose to speak to someone through dream and another through revelation and to another set of people it may be either voice or vision. Moses received a special grace from God in hearing from Him (Exodus 33:17-20; Num 12:1-5) but not that he saw God physically. You can only see God in the eternity to come if you are so holy. Israel was chosen by God to hear directly from Him right from heaven in His own normal voice. (Exodus 20:19). *"For ask now concerning the days that are past which were before you, since the day that God created man on earth: and ask from one end of heaven to the other, whether any great thing like this has happened, or anything like it has been heard. Did any people ever hear the voice of God speaking out of the midst of the fire as you have heard and live"(Deut. 4:3236).*

The same God of the ancient times who spoke to Abraham, Isaac and Jacob is still speaking today to Christians who are ready and willing to obey His instruction.

The mystery of God's voice is that, it is not all voices you hear that are direct voice of God Almighty (Heb. 1:1-2). Even from ancient time, God has been speaking through His angels, His son, Holy Ghost, prophets and personally. Don't be confused about this that all the messages will be addressed after God because He is the Sender (Exodus 3:2-4). If you carefully observe this verse, you will discover that the verse two started with angel and when it comes to verse four the Lord saw the action of Moses and God appeared to him. Any messages delivered by any one of them should be addressed as to God because He is the Source of the message. Whoever that want to hear God's voice must be ready to obey God and give his life to Him and receive His Spirit (Acts 5:32; Jn 4:24). Message to preach and prayer to pray but they starts copying another man's vision.

Once we have known that the church of God is a living church, we must try to learn on how to have a relationship with God. Learn to be in His presence always. A man that is lonely with God always will never be short of His message (Psalm 91:1-10).

Sinners cannot be hearing from God always but God can only speak to them on their salvation or on what that can take their life away because God does not want anybody to perish (Jn 3:16).

We have a lot of factors that determines constancy in hearing from God which includes the following:

1. Reading of God's Word always
2. Praying constantly
3. Often fasting and prayer
4. Diligence (Deut. 28:1-8).
5. Heart of expectation when waiting upon Him.
6. Humility must be your order of the day.

Many have chosen wrong alternative choice for themselves because they cannot hear directly from God. There is a need for a ladder of faith to hear from Him always. We must possess His Spirit to be able to hear from Him always. It is only a spiritual man that can be so closer to the mind of God. The voice of Almighty God may come to you like the voice of human being like the case of Samuel in the book of 1 Samuel 3:7-10 but it will only take a matured Christian to understand or recognize the voice of God from other voices.

How to recognize the voice of God from other voices: Believe it that our God is not an author of confusion as said in His word (1 Cor 14:33). But you can know His words remains infallible. The word of God can never change (Ps 62:11). Once He speaks, it remain established forever. He can choose to speak to you through biblical verses or word. He can choose to speak to others through some real man of God's picture they know physically. The more He gains your attention towards Himself the more He desire to speak to you either in your prayer closet or in your dreams. Manipulation can occur whenever you are doing wrong things or when you fail to pray at all times.

There is a way to respond to God's voice not arrogantly, like Cain (Gen 4:6-13), Saul (1 Sam 13:11) and Eli (1 Sam 3:18). Brethren, it is high time we know that God Almighty is more than our biological father and He is not anyway our mate. We must also recognize that God do normally speak in part. This is to tell us that we cannot know all things about our life at a time from God (I Cor 13:9). Paul heard the voice of God on his way to Damascus and God did not tell him what to do but rather He said He will send Anania the prophet to him (Acts 9:1-15). We must not play or joke with His voice but let us make sure we give respect to His voice. We can confirm the voice of God by asking Him to give us signs like Gideon (Judges 6:17, 36-40) and He can choose to give us a negative sign or even punishment if we are not specific or if we disbelieve Him like Zachariah in Luke 1:18, and Abraham in Gen 15:8. John the Baptist was demoted and deprived of his heavenly and eternity position as a result of his doubting during trials of life. (Matt 11:1-11).

Advantages of Hearing from God

* It always keeps us away from digression and from going astray from the purpose of God.
* It always promotes and actualize our security
* The more you hear from God the more you fulfil your destiny. If you don't know how to respect God and His anointed one, you cannot gain His honour and also His anointing cannot work for you.
* Ability to hear from God will give confidence and boldness on your vision and your mission.
* Hearing from Him always resulted in independent act.

CHAPTER 9
WAITING FOR YOUR TIME

Time is changing in season that has to do with hours, minutes and seconds. The word of God has respect for time. One of the greatest things in the world today that the astronomers are taking into consideration is time. One of the basic things that controls weather forecast in every places is change in the time. God created everything in respect with time (Eccl. 3:11; Gen1:31). You cannot change the time but you can only change to time. Time is one of the major things that always dictate what to do as regards human endeavour that we must all patiently wait and study in order to succeed in life.

There is time for everything in life (Eccl. 3:1-8). We have times for planting and also for expectation and also time to harvest. If you are planning in dry season you will later end up in wasting your time and resources. There is a time to wake-up, time to work, time to rest and time to sleep. All these should not be misused by anybody less he/she find him/herself in the grave. Everything God did was in order or arrangement with time and even times for Him Self also (Gen 2:1-3).

A waste of time is a waste of life and resources. One of the major problem we are facing today is that we are not fulfilling at the normal time. We must try to understand that the creation was programmed in respect with time (Gen 8:22) and failing to know this will amount to our failure in life. Many would have been a great man/woman today in their endeavour, but they failed to do the normal thing at the normal time. What a great loss in the life of Gehaz who failed to recognize the time to give out and the time to receive. He took gifts when he supposed to tarry in God's presence (2 Kgs 5:26). May you not do such in Jesus name. Many want to be a leader, master and teacher without being a servant, apprentice and student. Show me fulfilled men/women, they are men and women who are time conscious (Eccl 9:11). You must try to study the type of work you are doing may be it is a seasonal job that will not take care of your family tomorrow.

It is not the day that Jacob received the last blessing from his father that Esau failed (Gen 27:39-42). But he has failed right from the day he was unable to withstand the hunger of some hours mainly because he wanted to satisfy his appetite for a while and decided to sold his birthright that stood for his everlasting heritage and glory (Gen 25:30-34). Don't be a fool when it comes to foolish things and don't ever take an irrational decision when you are confused for a while it can jeopardize your life.

Many great men and women of God have disappointed God just because of unusual sexual urge. Though David was forgiven by God not to die but he brought a heavy punishment on Israel up till today, just because he was at the wrong place at a wrong time and slept with another man's wife to satisfy his sexual desire for just a moment and he lost a great honour (2 Sam 11:15). Don't ever go alone and visit a sister in the home at the wrong time of the day. Be aware that God is watching over your life and the time given to you in life both the secret time and your public time.

Every manifestation in life is tied down with a particular time. Whoever that want to win a race must be time conscious. Winning in a race doesn't depend on personal skill and talent alone but really on accuracy with time. Your fall and die prayer can only work for you whenever it is uttered at the normal time.

No pregnant woman can decide on her issue of delivery ahead of the normal delivery time in the name of "I don't have time". The time of life cannot change for anybody but you can change to time.

CHAPTER 10
TIME OF MANIFESTATION

There is time for manifestation of God's glory in every man's life, and don't ever mess up your time with another man's time. John the Baptist was well equipped for God's work before embarking on it. (Lk 1:80).

Many ministers today want to start their ministry in a day and arrived in the same day not thinking of the appointed time of manifestation. This is the main reason behind untimely death of many ministers attending to what their power is not enough to conquer (Jn 14:14).

Allow God to usher and launch your destiny to glorious explosion of power by taking time to know your time and stop envying and jealousy others because they are manifesting.

Rome was not built in a day; you need to know your own time. Jesus Christ was expected by His mother to perform miracles because she knew He could do it (Jn 2:2-5) but He responded by telling her to respect time order for manifestation. Don't play with your time because you cannot exchange anything for it. Oh you sinner, you only have a little opportunity for being alive to listen to this Word and it is highly important for you to give your life to Christ and stop sinning because your repentance may be too late (Eccl 12:1-9).

Unfortunately, Esau, Judas Iscariot, and Saul repented lately and it was not accepted (Gen 27:38; Matt 27:1-10; Acts 1:1719).

Delaying in time can affect God's agenda on man's glory and that is the main reason why you must work for God at the normal time that you have the opportunity to do so (Eccl 9:10; Col 3:23-24). Amount of wasted time will amount to man's destiny. Don't ever be busy on unnecessary thing. Don't allow television, home theatre, social media, phones and computer to take away your important time of busying with God.

Keep your quiet time intact, your fasting time and time to study His Word.

CHAPTER 11
ABILITY TO DECIDE AFTER GOD'S CONVICTION

Whoever that takes a step after God's decision will not end up being failure. When you decide without the decision of Almighty God, you are bound to be a failure. It is also a strong-will-power to dominate over other suggestion, idea, instruction and advice. It is also to exercise uncompromised mind on any given thought. We have a lot of good vision, and dreams unaccomplished in many believers' lives today because of indecision. Beloved, I am telling us to develop a heart of possibility in everything we are committed to do or committed to our care. People love to carry people along whenever they want to decide or embark on a new vision after God's conviction.

Once Paul was called into the ministry he did not dialogue with anybody but went straight to obey the heavenly vision just the way God is talking to you today that you are saying that you need another man's conviction (Gal. 1:16). Many that are not pleasing God today are those people who are not ready to take step after God's instruction. Abraham wouldn't have become a father of faith, if he had dialogue with his wife on the offering of Isaac as a sacrifice unto God that resulted to his entrusted as a friend of God. (Gen. 22:1-3).

You can also be a friend of God like Abraham (2 Chron 20:7; Isa 41:8; Jn 15:14; James 2:23). The instruction of God Almighty is that you should not join multitude to do evil (Exo 23:2). There is no amount of excuses you can present to God that will justify your faults. Saul brought the anger of God upon himself when he failed to execute God's instruction because of the influence of the multitude on his decision and later became a fool in the sight of God (1 Sam 15:24). It is not wise to say "experience is the best teacher" but is rightly approved to say "example is the best teacher". Whatever you want to do in life, do it and don't say nobody has done it before you.

See yourself as somebody that can be an example to others. Eve was able to change the mind of Adam on God's given instruction despite the fact that he heard from God directly but he could not help himself out of the situation until he finished completely because of his-low-will power to stand on God's decision and instruction (Gen 3:6). Let me tell you that you cannot succeed until you develop a heart of independency in decisionmaking after God's approval.

Many have turned away from God's instruction, original calling, initial instruction, early pattern and vision of their ministry through the influence of other backslidden pastors, leaders or modern day preacher. Many cannot even decide again on their own until there is prophecy from other brethren or somebody else in the church. Don't be deceived if any message comes to you in the name of the Lord.

You must try to go back to God that spoke to you earlier in order not to miss the original track like the young prophet sent to Bethel (1 Kgs 13:1-18) which listened to the voice of a backslider prophet and died miserably. There is nothing a man has become in life that you cannot become and there is nothing a man possess in life that you cannot possess in as much you can make a positive decision on every given instruction from God. Believe me, heaven is your limit! You can never decide if you don't stop listening to what people will say or what people will do. What matters is what God will say or do. Your ability can only be known when you prove it to people by action.

As a real believer, you must be independent, if you are dealing with God. We have a lot of problems that are causing inability to decide personally when dealing with God. There is something we called "inner drive" which is ability to respond to a necessary event naturally. If God is not realizing His aim of speaking to His people, there will be problem of discontinuity in our relationship with Him as a result of all these problems.

a. **Fear:** To be fearful is to be in danger or risk of doing things. It is also a terrible weapon in the hand of the devil to deal with a compromise Christians. The Bible declares that fear has a torment and it normally withers the hand of Almighty God from fighting for someone. Sometimes we are scared as a result on inexperience (Judges 8:21; Eph 4:14). If you are in fear you will not be able to exercise your lordship authority. Fear can put someone in bondage. An intimidation may cause fear for someone (2 Tim 1:7; Rom 8:15). In several places in the Bible, wherever the angel of the Lord appears to His people because of his fierce physique, he would need to declare that you should not be "fearful" (Jer 1:8). God sovereignty is all over places, He will not fear anybody or any situation. As children of God, you don't need to fear anybody but you can only respect people (Acts 13:46; 4:31; 4:13; Dan 3:18). One of the major things that give devil permission to torment Job was "fear" (Job 3:25). Let me tell you that there is no faith in fear. When you are fearful you are bound to be defeated by devil and his agents. God cannot do anything for you apart from your faith and devil cannot do anything against you apart from your fear.

b. **Inferiority Complex:** It is a strong feeling of incapability of doing normal things of life. What you think about yourself matters a lot and it will always determine how people will address you. Don't ever think negative about yourself. The Word of God says we are fearfully and wonderfully created. Look at the Word of God for your life and know the promises of God for your life that you are not ordinary but god among men (Isa 43:3-6; 1 Peter 2:9; Ps 105:14-15; 125:3; 45:7).

C. Unbelief or Doubt: Lest you forget, unbelief will never allow someone to achieve his/her goal even though he/she is hearing from

God every day. Inability to take a positive step after God's conviction may come as a result of our unbelief. You can overcome this by going back to God in your prayer closet (James 1:6).

Chapter12
YOU NEED TO KNOW MORE

We must not be thinking parochially as Christians. It must be known to us that; it is good for a Christian to have an enlarged heart towards spiritual things. Apostle Paul said that he has never attained and arrived (Phil 3:13). We must not be satisfied with our present spiritual state. Let us aspire to know more about our God, have you finished reading the whole Bible once in year? Try to re-read again (Phil 3:10). You are there and you have received the Holy Spirit, thinking that it is enough. No! It is not enough for you. What have you done that you are complaining about prayer and fasting whereas Jesus Christ was God and yet He still prayed as if He was not God.

We must desire spiritual gifts as Paul said in his book (1 Cor 14:1). God is really expecting us to metamorphose from babyhood to adulthood (Heb 6:1-2). Don't ever see yourself as somebody that has arrived neither see yourself as someone who has made it all. Let me tell you that you haven't known anything but little. Apostle Paul who was filled with abundant of revelations and he was still agitating (Eph 3:17-19). The more you know about God, the more you dominate your environment and everything put into you care. Lest you forget today that you only know little about God Almighty. You can prove that you know Him until you are known and you cannot be known until when you know Him.

Many Christians today are just like the Ephesian disciples who were following Christ without deeper knowledge of the full gospel and they were with titles, position and activities in the church (Acts 19:1-6). When you know little about God, you cannot deliver much. We have a lot of preachers and Christians who could not interpret the Old Testament scriptures talk less of application. Try to study your bible as if you are going for an examination ahead.

Many are so confused about the Bible and many cannot identify the truth from ordinary profane words. You need to be rooted in God's Word in order not to be deceived by any erroneous teachers, prophets and so-called men of God. Apostle Paul was able to fish out a girl who was doing the work of God with sorcery spirit which is called syncretism.

It is not every tongue that comes from God, please try to discern it today in your church (Acts 16:16-18). It is because you know little about God that is why people and devil are maneuvering you like novice.

Many could not even differentiate the mind of God from traditional law or custom and medical assessment together with human philosophical idea. The more you know will determine judge rightly between two ministers that are doing normal things and otherwise in the name of grace, mercy and calling. But try to know this today that our God is not a respecter of anybody, the way you serve Him will determine how you are going to enjoy Him (1 Peter 1:17; Rom 2:11; Acts 10:34). Whatsoever that He will not allow from Bro "A" He will not take it from Bro "B".

You cannot know anything until you belief that you don't know anything at all. In as much there is vacuum, there must be provision or release of divine benefits from God until when there is no space to contain it again. This is the mystery of "more" from God (2 Kgs 4:1-6). This divine provision stopped when there was no available vessel. Likewise, whoever that sees him/herself as somebody that has arrived can never receive more.

Nobody can describe what he/she has never seen to somebody. Likewise, you cannot give what you don't have to people. You can only give what you have. What you know about God will determine what you will say about Him. Some people know God and they were filled with a measure of His Spirit and some know Him and they were filled with unmeasured and unlimited anointing (Ps 23:5).

Have you been to the level of thousand, try to go to millions level. What you know about God determine your spiritual greatness in God. At this juncture, we all need to sit down and examine ourselves, maybe we are still on the right track or not and if you are on the right track, you are in the normal position. You need to answer this question within yourself, how many lives have you been able to save?

Many have been tired, disturbed, discouraged and loosing inner urge of serving Him the more because of ephemeral things of this world (Prov 24:10).

Many who are graduates today in secular world are novice, dullard, moron, imbecile, and brutish when it comes to spiritual matters. How many revelations have you received about the Bible you are reading not even talking about your personal spiritual life whereas many have gone so far in making research on heavenly matters to ascertain their reality (2 Cor 12:1-4). What you know is not enough at all. While many of us should aspire to be teachers, masters, leaders, coordinators, pastors, deacons, deaconess, bishops and prophets, we are still looking for somebody to teach us the elementary Word of God and even looking for somebody to conduct deliverance for us (Heb 5:12-14). What a pity?

Brethren, we need to be more committed than ever before as we are moving closer to the close of this age. Are you part of those babies that knows little about God, spiritual matter and eschatological event? (1 Cor 3:1-4; 1 Peter 2:1-2). The expectation of God from your life is to be a teacher of His people (Jn 21:15; Jer 3:15). For how long are you going to stay at a point? What have you done for God since you have been in the Christendom? Don't deceive yourself, if rapture take place today, can you receive any reward at the Bema Seat or haven't you heard of it that there are rewards for the Christians who labour much for God after knowing Him. As you know all the name of inventors, philosophers and historical men, try to know all the characters in the Bible and make sure the word of God is settled in your heart and endeavour to recite your Bible off-hand (Col. 3:16).

We need to move forward to higher level. God is taking a lot of people to higher ground if only they can surrender all unto God absolutely. Before we can take the gospel of Christ to all the parts of the world, we must move from well of living water to a river or ocean of the living water to its fullness.

Well of living water (Jn 4:14) to river of living water (Jn 7:38), and to its fullness (Ezek 47:4). Coming up higher is a message that deals with exploits. We should not limit our thinking on the things of this world alone but we should be heavenly conscious and set our affection on the things of God (1 Pet 1:4) *"If in this life only we have hope in Christ, we are of all men most miserable"* (I Cor 15:19). God want to move our lives from stagnancy to upper room because there are rooms in the higher places. Jesus Christ told His disciples that they should not be troubled that in His Father's house there are many mansions (Jn 14:1-3). If you are at the top, climax, peak and upper level, you can easily gaze up and see clearly everything at the lower or down level. And if you are not careful, you may think that you have made it all not knowing that there are rooms at the top. To maintain the top or higher position, you need to pay some prices and make some sacrifices.

Many were born to be great and many want to be great but only few can pay the price to be great and maintain the greatness. The power of God is unlimited and dynamic. We should not think in a stereotyped way when dealing with God Almighty. We need an abundant of revelation to move our life forward. While waiting on God many lives have come across the secret of God's greatness. Why should we wait till we die? You need to move forward and regain your spiritual strength and boldness. Don't be a lazy person if you want to know more about God. If you really want to know more, you must learn how to wait on God in prayer. Many that supposed to take their generation from poverty or deliver their generation from calamity like Joseph have compromised and failed to know more. Daniel was able to get an access into the spirit-world because he chose to wait on God and mystery was revealed to him (Dan 9:10-15. We need to wait on God (Isa 40:31; 25:9; 30:18; Ps 40:1-4).

Chapter13
PLEASING GOD

In whatever we are doing in life, we must ensure that we are pleasing God and not man. But many are men pleaser. They will be expecting what people will say concerning them. Are you living to please friends, parent, relatives and leaders? Let me tell you that you cannot serve God and the same time serve devil. You must please one and forsake the other one (Col 3:23-24; Eph 6:6-7). It is a great thing for God to be well pleased with you as He was pleased with Jesus Christ (Matt. 3:17; 17:5).

We can only last in reigning as a leader of His Kingdom if we please Him thoroughly in all the days of our lives. The kingdom of some kings could not last in the Old Testament mainly because they could not please God (2 Chron 24:2; 264; 27:2; 29:2).

If God does not delight in you, you are just wasting your time in His presence. Jesus Christ said whoever that loves either father or mother more than Him is not worthy of His own. Don't be a hypocrite to be seen of men in anything you are doing in life (Matt 6:1-6). God cannot be mocked; whatever you sow you shall reap. Don't desire to satisfy human being but try to please your

Maker in all things that He may reward you accordingly.

Judas Iscariot was following Jesus Christ not because he loved the gospel but because of his selfish interest. Likewise, today, many are coming into the church not because they really love the gospel but because of one thing or the other they are still available, but let them find what they are looking for; they will not come to church again. Are you part of this people? Check yourself, the end is near.

Don't serve God because of anything but serve God because He is your Maker and He is worthy to be praised, served, and worshiped. To please God is to do what is right before God with a perfect intent of heart. If you are trying to please men, you will end up in displeasing yourself.

CHAPTER 14
THE FEAR OF THE LORD

To fear God is to depart from evil and living a sinless life and not to be gentle or cool in the face. To fear God is not to be gentle in the church alone and remain as lion at home. You can only be known as somebody that fears God when you keep to all His precept and instruction.

To fear God is to obey every of His word to letter. The Book of Proverbs chapter one verse seven says *"The fear of the LORD is the beginning of knowledge: but fools despise wisdom and instruction"*. Acceptance of Christ Jesus, the "Wisdom" and the "Power of God" according to I Cor 1:24 is an assurance of His fear. Are you acquainted with His Word? That is the beginning of wisdom but you must continue reading your Bible that represents the Wisdom (Ezra 7:25) if really you want to prove that you fear Him truly.

Show me a man who has never forsaken his/her sins, claiming that he fears God, maybe he is morally okay or full of activities in the church he doesn't fear God! (Prov 8:13; Job 1:1; Prov 16:6). The Pharisees believed that they fear of God but they normally give respect to His name but their heart was so far from Him (Isaiah 29:13). Coming to church does not prove that you fear Him. It is those people who gives regard to His entire commandment that He believed that they really fear Him.

Are you part of those people that are coming to His presence with boy and girl friends giving excuses in obeying Him perfectly? That is the major reason while you are losing a lot of benefits that belong to those people who fear Him every day.

You cannot fear God and yet remain in darkness concerning His secret (Ps 25:14). The angel of the living God cannot fail to perform their normal duty/service in protecting those people who fear God (Ps 34:7). Long life and old age are apportioned for the fearful children (Prov 10:27) and God can never deprive them of good things of life (Prov 22:4; 23:17). It is highly important that we must fear Him so as to enjoy His unlimited blessing for the rest our lives.

CHAPTER 15
IGNORING THE PAST

This message is coming to all Christians teaching us to live a life of forgiveness and forgetfulness not minding the gravity of what might have happened in the past. You need to purge out all these obnoxious thought out of your life and be ready for God for a new virtue. God spoke to Moses in Exodus 3:5 saying "... *Draw not high hither: put off thy shoes from off thy feet, for the place whereon thou standest is holy ground"*. You cannot receive a new vision for your life and your generation without ignoring the past. Your assignment cannot receive all your attention until you forget everything about yourself and past. Your past cannot stop your future from manifesting likewise you must decide on how to forget everything that will not allow you to think about your future.

Many are still carrying the scar of what has happened when they were yet to give their lives to God. Some are thinking on the atrocities they have committed in the past even though they have submitted their lives to God but they still have their unforgettable imagination which is detrimental to their immediate success. It doesn't matter where you are from but where you are going to is what really matters to God. The Old Testament was a mirror and a shadow of the original testimony which is the New Testament. Don't ever join those people who are still carrying the Old Testament doctrine that Jesus has put an end to *"How much more shall the blood of Christ, who through the eternal Spirit offered himself without spot to God, purge your conscience from dead works to serve the living God…?* (Heb 9:14-17). It is necessary that we should renew our mind from every pattern of the world so as to please God (Rom 12:1). What are you still carrying about that can jeopardize your future assignment? Try to purge them off from your mind. You can only move little when you are still carrying one burden or heaviness in your heart. And darkness can remove you totally in this Christian race, if you don't change. Solomon has never taken time in his life time to condemn himself nor his destiny about how he was born nor his parent marital status. What he believed that made him to excel was his believing in the plan of Almighty God for him. Try to clear off your mind from all those things you are thinking about, believe that whosoever that is in Christ Jesus is a new creature and behold all things are new (2 Cor 5:17). Knowing this as a fact that your mind is carrying all the vision of your life.

CHAPTER 16
KEYS TO SUCCESSFUL LIFE

We have a lot of things which constitute an outstanding life, you can only be addressed as a successful man/woman when you are complete in all facet of life. Belief that all these things are been ordered by GOD Himself. There are six areas of life: marital, metaphysical, material, academic, relationship and financial life,

Financial life:

We should try to understand that most of the important and inevitable parts of the body are not even recognized at time (1 Cor 12:14-26). To be financially buoyant is to have a capacity to be responsible for necessary needs. Poor is the name to qualify whoever that is not capable to be responsible financially to meet their immediate need. To be poor is very painful and is one of the greatest pains that there is no curative medicine to eliminate. If there is no God's intervention at all, many dreams and vision would not have come true in life. Financial life is not the first in order of priority to GOD than to be saved but humanly speaking

Somebody like Moses who killed human fellow like himself would be relevant to the purpose of God? Not talking of his closeness to Almighty God after his encounter with God. Let me tell you, your past mistakes cannot disturb or affect your future if you can be with God throughout the days of your life.

We need to be rich in order to meet up with the standard of living in the society. Everything said in the Bible about the riches is purely good. Money is very small but it answers all things. It means as small as it is, it has been a major thing that is controlling all other aspect of life.

The Bible talks about the rich people which people loves to be their friend (Pr 14:20; 19:4, 7) and the poor are hated by all people. We should not be confused about the mind of Jesus Christ on the rich people. To be rich is not a sin and it cannot take us to hell when is being utilized well according to the mind of God. It is not wealth that took the rich man to hell during the time of Lazarus. Likewise, the proverb of Jesus Christ should not be misapplied (Mk 10:23-27; Lk 16: 19 -25), we don't need to leave the weightier matters and pursue money or riches when we haven't given our life to God.

God is the owner of riches (Hag 2:8), let God bless you richly; you will discover that to be rich is more honorable in society than to be poor. The poor is being enslaved by the rich. When the rich are ruling over the poor, it will not allow the poor to exercise their normal right (Pr 22:7). Inferiority complex will always be coming when you have an idea without money to execute it. There is nothing that is good in life than to have an ability to provide for our necessary needs.

Riches always create a different mentality to an individual that possess it but don't allow riches to make you proud. Solomon made a very serious message on poverty and riches (Pr 30:8-9). It worth discussing my brethren; this is the main reason while the gospel of Christ was being preached to the poor that they may receive their liberation (Matt 11:5). It is the mind of God that we should be rich because of His death. Really, the Bible described those people who cannot provide for their family as somebody who is so worse than unbeliever. That will not be our portion in Jesus name.

We must learn how to be financially independent as an individual Christian so as to provide for our family. Paul said whoever that is not ready to work should not eat (2 Thess 3:10). One of the weapon of judgment is famine. It is as painful to be a victim of hunger strike, this is why we must develop a habit of not depending on our income. How can we be financially independent except we learn how to handle some personal business? Everybody cannot get white collar job. And one of the real problem both in a state and in a country as a whole is unemployment. At every successful business, there is a risk. Don't ever think that you will not face one challenge or the other if you own a personal business. You can also be an agricultural investor by embarking on agricultural production. You can start home lesson for children and later it may yield to a bigger school.

We must also possess business orientation. It is very good for us to learn a hand work so as to support our daily living financially. We can established ourselves, if we are so ready to become an independent marketer with the little token we have at hand. Also we need to empower our member who is hardworking in order to be independent by lending them money.

Spiritual life:

This is a life that is relevant to the purpose of God. When you are yet to give your life to Christ, you are nobody irrespective of what you have achieved in life. Spiritual life is a way of relating with God. Your relationship with God will determine your eternity. We must learn how to relate with our God. But you need to know the secret of His relationship. We need to be closer to God in His word and in prayer. These two keys control the spiritual aspect of every life. To be closer to God as a friend is so much admirable than to be beggar in His presence.

Your constancy in His presence will bring down His presence closer to you every day. If you are reading the Bible alone, you cannot be feeling His presence every day. Please learn how to be tarrying in His presence for effective communication. Believe me that "prayer' is not to ask nor rebuke demons but a means of communication between man (in physical flesh) and God (in spirit). Listen, every human being carries a percentage of spirit and together with the help of Holy Spirit, you can move easily into the realm of the spirit to commune with the Spirit of Almighty God. Talking to God is called prayer, either you close your eyes or not, may be you are speaking loudly or within (Jn 4:24). There are lots of ways to approach the throne of God through prayer that we can term to be kinds of prayer. Try to understand the place of fasting in every prayer we are praying. Fasting is an empowerment to our spiritual life in order to keep the spirit strong and powerful to be sensitive to all spiritual message and feelings. A natural man cannot understand the things of the Spirit as the Bible declares. As we have different kinds of messages and feeling through vision, dream and revelation as in message of relationship, rebuking correction, and instruction. Likewise, we have different kinds of prayer to receive kinds of answers. I will like to mention and explain some that are so important to us. They are prayer of adoration, prayer of petition, prayer of thanksgiving, prayer of warfare, prayer of deliverance, prayer of supplication, prayer of consecration, prayer of inquiring and prayer of authority. Prayer of agreement as part of the kinds of prayer, prayer of forgiveness, prayer of expectation and prayer of intercession. You are not spiritual until you pray according to the mind of God. We must possess a perfect understanding about kinds of prayer so as to know the right word and steps to take whenever we are in the presence of God. What many call prayer is not prayer but noise.

a. <u>Prayer of Adoration:</u>

This is when you reference God and you bless His name and shower encomium on Him to glorify His majesty. This is not to come to the presence of God and start embarrassing Him and raise offences against Him thinking by this He would answer quickly. When you make God to realize Himself and His position in your life, He will do more than your expectation (1 Chron 29:10). Jehoshaphat blessed God by starting with all His glorious and wonderful deeds in the Bible and suddenly the message came to them and the Lord surprised them as never before (2 Chron 20:20). Will you praise Him today and bless His name and stop complaining, murmuring and grudging about?

b. <u>Prayer of petition:</u>

It is a formal request to God to take a particular action. This is when things are going on contrary to what the authority has written. It seems like a report or as if you are lodging complain on man issue specified before. Elijah made a prayer of petition against the people of Israel when they were committing sin, yet they were enjoying all the benefits of God and he prayed that there should be no rain for three and half years (2 kings 17:1-5; 2 Chron 24:27).

c. <u>Prayer of thanksgiving :</u>

To thank somebody on the past benefits always attract new benefits. Whereas when dealing with God you must have the same mind. Jesus blessed God at the sepulcher of Lazarus not because He cannot authorized but to show to people the importance of thanksgiving in prayer expectation (Jn 11:35-40). Paul said we should be giving thanks in all things (1 Thess 5:18). Saying it is the will of God (Ps 103:1-3). Learn how to bless Him always for all His wonderful and marvelous deeds.

d. <u>Prayer of warfare:</u>

Knowing fully well that our God is a Chief Commander of armed forces in the heavenly places, He is a Chief Warrior and we too must act like Him by not fearing devil and his agents. Devil always respect a relative prayer made on the altar of holiness. Before you can wage war against devil, you must humble yourself under the mighty hand of God. This is to obey to letter all the spiritual messages from your physical leader and also obey God's Word (James 4:7). Then the devil will flee from you. Belief me that prayer of warfare is a merciless prayer and also a desperate prayer that carries an authority with expectation. It is always full of fall and dies address. It is also a prayer of spiritual attack against the kingdom of darkness in charge of the so-called predicament (2 Cor 10:3-4; Eph 6:11-12). These two scriptures are common but serious verse in the Bible that should be addressed with serious attention. Warfare prayer is a prayer of fighting, seeing God as the Chief Host of the battle. Then you must not slack, relent, relax and sluggish but be vigilant and raise up your spiritual antenna because devil will reinforce back. It should be full of boldness and aggression. Please note this is the secret of warfare prayer. You don't talk too much, or crack jokes when praying nor waste time when you know that devil is at hand or when God is giving a lot of revelation of battle (negative revelation) (Jn 14:30). Ministers, don't take it for granted. An aggressive prayer will bring God's attention.

e. Prayer of deliverance:

This is a spiritual utterance to loose someone inner man from a spiritual bondage. It is also to come out from a spiritual prison. Prayer that call for detachment of strange people and strange things. One of the powerful weapons to achieve this is anointing fire of Almighty God. If you want to go far in life, you need to put off some wrong things from your life and even wrong people that will not allow you to achieve your vision. You need to pass through deliverance in order for you to come out of those spiritual entanglements you find yourself. You need freedom from the power of oppression, depression and obsession. If you really want to be delivered, you need to be free from sin (Obadiah 17-18) it is also to save some from the danger of life.

f. Prayer of supplication:

This is when we are asking God to do something particular in our life. We are admonished to present our request before God. Whatever we ask from God with faith shall be granted (James 1:6-7).

g. Prayer of consecration:

It is a prayer of dedication in order to separate oneself from the worldly things and pleasure. Job made a covenant with God not to behold virgin (Job 31:1) this is to make commitment with God and to pray to please God.

h. Prayer of enquiry:

This is to pray and received the mind of God concerning a particular matter. It is a questioning prayer whereby you need to ask God one by one in order to avoid error in answer. It is also to give a directive on a particular matter. You need to be so sure that God has spoken to you before taking any step at all. We cannot know all things at once but when we are so close to God, it shall be perfectly revealed to us. This type of prayer is very important when one is to embark on any project or journey or decision (1Sam10:22; 2Chron 18:7; 2kings 3:11-13; 1 Sam 30:7).

i. Prayer Of Authority:

It is a prayer of establishment to possess a place. This is to use bible quotations to establish the mind of God.

j. Prayer of agreement:

This is to agree with one or two or more people in prayer concerning a matter (Matt 18:18-20).when you agree with somebody in prayer, you must be very careful with the person you will agree with during prayer time. Prayer of agreement always empowers someone who is so weak in the spirit (prov. 27:17). It always encourages us to pray more when seeing people to join us in the time of prayer.

k. <u>Prayer of forgiveness:</u>

One of the greatest prerequisites to every answered prayer is to forgive others in prayer. Prayer of forgiveness is to forgive others too (Lk 11:4; Matt 6:12 -15; 18:23-35). Prayer of forgiveness is a prayer of soberness and brokenness in the presence of God. You must esteem yourself lower than what you think you are. It is very good at earlier of every prayer in order to clear our conscience from all guiltiness of heart and condemnation of heart. At times, many normal pray a prayer of forgiveness not because they are still committing sin but to humble themselves before God and count themselves not to be righteous though they are righteous. Please note, it may not be compulsory at times when the spirit of God or situation doesn't permit us to do so. When you receive forgiveness from God through your prayer then you will gain an access to God's benefits (healing, miracle, salvation etc.)

l. <u>Prayer of expectation:</u>

An act of expectation is to await a result of expected case. It is also to be looking forward for a particular result with eagerness. It is also to build faith concerning a matter to be seen and having an assurance surely that it will manifest no matter the case may be. Expectation can be expressed as to put all totality of heart and mind on an incoming result. Expectation doesn't cast away hope but putting firmly together the state of mind in positive direction. Expectation always works with faith (Mk 5:31-34) we also have "great expectation" that always comes with divine mercy, you must conclude that God will surely do it when praying for anything at all. Prayer of expectation always brings eagerness, aggression, violent and irresistible faith. You must always be in the mood of receiving it. This doesn't prove that God will show how He will do it like Naman.

m. Prayer of intercession:

It has always been in the interest of Almighty God that people should fill-in some necessary gap for some people (Ezek 22:30). Intercession is to use your influence to bail others out of their pathetic situation. It is very costly and tasking in all aspect. Intercessor are filled with compassion and passion for other souls in problem and they are neither self-centered nor egocentric in nature. This is when you carry the burden of others in prayer to the presence of Almighty God. Moses, Samuel and Jeremiah believed that their relationship with God must influence others even to the extent that they don't mind their own. They are prayers offered on behalf of people to seeing them being well satisfied (Exo 32:32; 1 Sam 12:23; Jer 15:110). It must be prayed well as if you are the victim.

1. Ministerial Life:

When you are saved, you are expected to carry God's burden on yourself. For the fact that you are not a part-time or fulltime minister doesn't prove that you don't have a ministry. The purpose of Holy Ghost baptism is to empower Christian to carry out ministerial duties (Acts 1:8). Though there is five-fold ministry but it is not until you carry one title or the other that you are to be useful for God. Whatsoever you discover that you can do easily or seeing yourself doing in the dream always is your area of your specialization or ministerial assignment.

2. <u>Martial Life:</u>

Many homes are not settled and yet they are still calling themselves Christians. If you don't succeed in your marital life, you cannot be useful for God in the ministry (1 Tim 3:4). Marital success has to do with understanding of the both party. When you understand your partner, there will be no problem at all. One of the root causes of problem in marriage is, many marriages are not ordained by God. Many married as an unbeliever before they later got converted. Some married to unbeliever in the name of *"I will convert him/her"*. Many conclude that they will not fornicate but they are not ready to leave their boy/girlfriend. If you really want to be successful martially, there is need for you to study vividly what you discover that the other opponent hates most and what he/she like most. It is then you can live together in peace. As a man/woman, we must try as much as possible to put our homes together. We must not allow anything to put apart our first love. Please don't allow anybody to scatter your family in the name of "counsel" and we should not allow influence of our family to dominate our own family in the name of *"they are parent, sisters, brothers and we have known each other before I got married"*. Belief me sincerely, that you are going to give account of everything you are doing in life.

There are lots of things that dictate success in marriage. It is not when you wed that you are accounted to be successful. You need to study your spouse's weaknesses in order to help him/her out of problems. Marriage should be an enjoyable thing. But many couples lack discretion in handling their spouse. And before we can enjoy our marriage, we need to be a source of help to other party in all his/her weaknesses. One of the mystery of marriage is an "acceptance" (Gen 1:22-23). You must accept him/her together with all his/her faulty side and try as much as possible to work on those weakness to sooth your mind.

Whoever you know that you need in your journey to succeed in life must be carried along wherever you are going to, no matter the disability. Things cannot work out well when you don't accept your spouse as him/her was created. Stop complaining about your spouse instead call on God and take a physical step to work on his/her weakness and not to desire another woman/man which will be accounted as sin for you.

The second thing we must recognize about marriage is pure/God's love. Both parties must love each other before they can enjoy themselves. We men must allow our wives to have a full responsibility. You must engage them in something. Let them feel that they are still part of the home. Don't render them impotent in the marriage because it will help them to be creative and develop their potential. Let them feel that they are responsible.

Though we men are the head, yet we must not Lord over our spouse instead we should be a help-mate to them in all things. Men are given the leadership role to play in our individual homes but we should try to understand that we are not created to reign over other fellow creatures (Gen 1:26) but to be a help-mate to our partner. If your spouse is so lower to your expectation, please try to work on that and raise him/her up in that specific area you noticed.

Your failure to understand this as a couple will bring lapses and pandemonium into your marriage. We must try as a man or woman of faith to be matured in our character because our moral behavior has a lot to do in our destiny. There are lots of learning we can deduce from Genesis 2:24. Leaving one's parent and cleaving unto each other has a mystery of total dependence to stir up your own personal personality that will assist you in building your home. You must understand also that it is not an excuse for keep relationship with other people. Your exposure to people can bring blessings to you and curse also. There is what we call godly behavior (1 Tim 6:11), good behavior, elderly behavior (1 Tim 3:8), and holy behavior (1 Peter 1:15). Your action in the time of trouble and challenges will dictate your real man to people and also your genuineness of your faith to all Christians

From one generation to another we have discovered the importance of education in human life and also to the gospel. Right from the time of Adam, we have been having a lot of prophets but they were not so much useful because of their educational background until the time of Moses the prophet who was able to put down five books loaded with great divinity messages called ***"Pentateuch"*** (Acts 7:22), Moses was trained before he embarked on God's work. It will be so better for you if you have the opportunity of going to school and if you reject or refused it in the name of calling, that is foolishness and ignorance. It is very helpful in the gospel propagation because the Bible comes to us in different languages (Hebrew and Greek). The purpose of education in every country is not to add numbers together alone but also to solve the problems of language barriers. Academic impartation is to quicken our mental ability to understand things naturally and the understanding will bring knowledge of interpretation. We have a lot of Jews in Babylon Empire but Daniel was exceptional because of his academic background (Dan 1:4). In every academic pursuit, there are two major things that are so much important. These are reading and writing. Reading is an ability to spell out, pronounce written words correctly as it was written by the author (Hab 2:2a; Rev 1:3). Writing mean to put down correctly what a writer has in mind to the power of recognition

OTHER BOOKS BY PROPHET D.K. AKINBOYE

THE BREAKING SERMON AND SECURITY PRAYER

CONQUERING THE POWER OF SIN.

ESCAHTOLOGY BOOK

SECRET OF CHURCH GROWTH

About the Book

THE POWER OF RECOGNITION

To be highly recognized in heaven and on earth, you need to live a sacrificial life that will command the attention of people towards you.

This book has already taught us how to live a life that is full of indelible footprint. It has also shown us ways to become God's general with enviable characters.

About the Author

Prophet Daniel Kehinde Akinboye is a dynamic preacher of the Gospel rooted in the Bible with sound Prophetic ministry.

He is the founder of Joint Heirs of Salvation International Crusade Ministry. And also the provost of Daniel Prophetic International Bible College. He is married to Mrs. Blessing and blessed with Samuel and Joy.

He has authored a number of other publications including "Breaking Sermon and Security Prayer", "Prophetic Knowledge" and Secrets of Church Growth".

www.ingramcontent.com/pod-product-compliance
Lightning Source LLC
LaVergne TN
LVHW050340160826
845677LV00014B/3709

* 9 7 9 8 8 4 8 1 9 4 6 1 6 *